MEASURING OUR WORLD

by Jennifer Blizin Gillis

CONTENTS

Measuring Our World	2
Which Way Is It?	4
How Long Is It?	6
How Heavy Is It?	8
How Much Is There?	10
How Much Time Does It Take?	12
How Fast Is It?	14
Glossary	16
Index	16

Rourke
Educational Media

rourkeeducationalmedia.com

Measuring Our World

How big is this snake? Every day, we measure things around us. One way we measure is by comparing one thing to another.

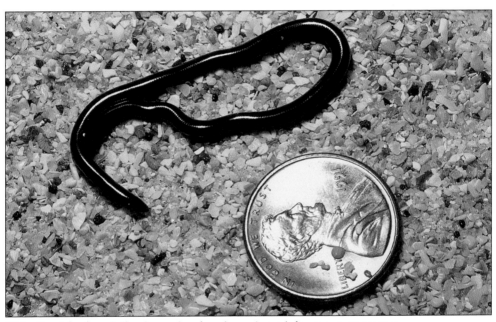

This Brahiminy blind snake is about as big as a penny.

A thermometer shows the temperature in degrees.

Another way to measure is to use an instrument, or tool. To learn how hot or cold something is, we use a thermometer. It is an instrument that measures temperature. We use many different instruments to help us measure.

Which Way Is It?

Some instruments show direction. You can use a compass to tell if you are facing or moving north, south, east, or west.

needle

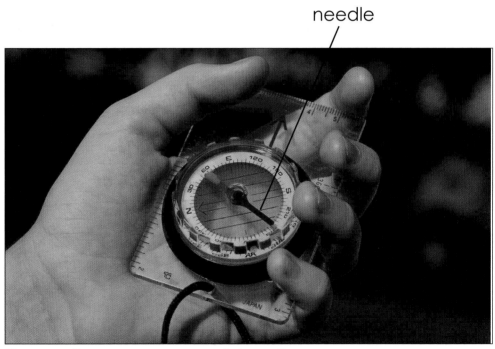

The needle on a compass points north.

A weathervane shows which way the wind is blowing. Part of the weathervane is like a compass. It shows north, south, east, and west. When the wind blows, the moving part of the weathervane—the arrow—points in the direction from which the wind is blowing.

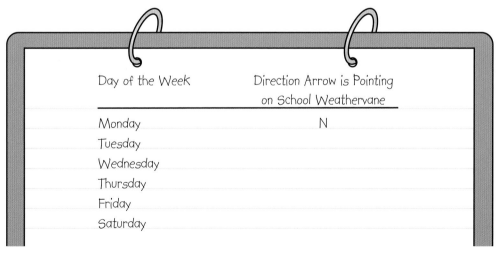

Day of the Week	Direction Arrow is Pointing on School Weathervane
Monday	N
Tuesday	
Wednesday	
Thursday	
Friday	
Saturday	

A sample student data sheet

How Long Is It?

A ruler shows how big this hailstone is in inches or millimeters.

You can measure how long or how wide something is with a ruler. The marks on the ruler show the units. Some marks show inches. Others show centimeters and millimeters. The marks are in the same places on every ruler. Most rulers are 12 inches long.

What if you need to measure something that is longer than 12 inches? You can use a measuring tape. One side of the tape is marked to show length in yards, feet, and inches. The other side is marked to show length in meters, centimeters, and millimeters.

These archaeologists are measuring the length of a part of an ancient building.

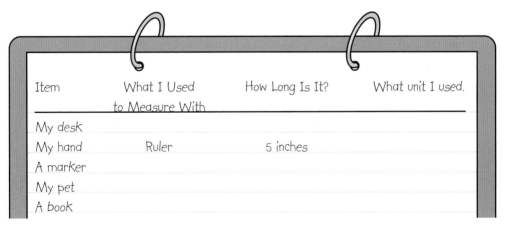

Item	What I Used to Measure With	How Long Is It?	What unit I used.
My desk			
My hand	Ruler	5 inches	
A marker			
My pet			
A book			

A sample student data sheet

How Heavy Is It?

There are two ways to weigh something. You can compare it to a known weight by using a balance. Like a see saw, when the weights are the same the balance is level.

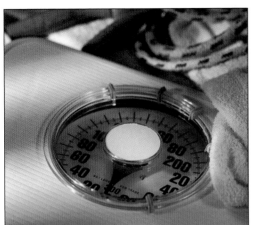

How much do you weigh?

Another way is to use an instrument that tells you the weight directly. You can use a bathroom scale to find your weight. The number of pounds will show on the dial.

Item I placed on a digital scale	How Much Does It Weigh?
Me	
My book bag	5 pounds
My pet	
My lunch	10 ounces
A book	

A sample student data sheet

How Much Is There?

In the kitchen, you can measure ingredients. A recipe tells you how much of each ingredient you will need. Measuring cups and spoons help you measure just the right amount of each ingredient.

This container measures volume, or how much is inside.

You might want to measure how much rain fell outside. A rain gauge is like a measuring cup that measures rain in inches. Rain falls into a container. The marks on the side of the container show how many inches of rain fell.

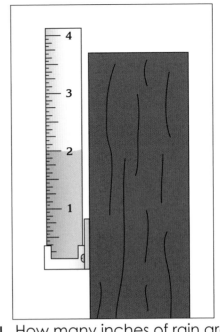

How many inches of rain are in the rain gauge?

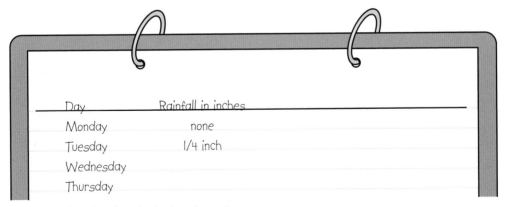

Day	Rainfall in inches
Monday	none
Tuesday	1/4 inch
Wednesday	
Thursday	

A sample student data sheet

How Much Time Does It Take?

Calendars divide a year into months and days. You can use a calendar to help you count how many months or days it will be until your birthday. People use calendars to help them measure long periods of time.

There are 12 months in a year. Some months have 31 days, and others have 30.

Clocks measure the time in seconds, minutes, and hours. Some clocks even tell you what day it is.

If you are making cookies, you do not want to use a calendar! You need to measure the time in smaller units like hours, minutes, or seconds.. A clock will help you measure the minutes the cookies need to bake in the oven.

Question	Time	What I Measured With
How long does it take to eat a cookie?		
How many days until your birthday?		
How long is the school day?	6 hours	A clock
How long is the school year?		
How long is recess?		

A sample student data sheet

How Fast Is It?

The runners on a track all go the same distance. The one who finishes in the shortest time is the fastest. And the winner!

If you want to measure speed, you need to know how far and how fast. You have to measure the distance and the time it takes to go that distance. Then you have to do some math. Speed is measured in units such as miles per hour.

Name	Time in seconds to run the 50 yard dash
Jake	34
Lane	
Tyler	
Maria	

A sample student data sheet

In a car, the speedometer shows how fast it is traveling. The numbers on the speedometer may go from 5 to 125. If the needle is on 40, the car is going at the rate of 40 miles in one hour.

GLOSSARY

balance instrument that measures using a beam or pole with a pan at each end

centimeter unit of measure in the metric system. A centimeter is about 0.39 inches or the width of your index finger.

ingredient one part of a mixture. Sugar is one ingredient in a cake.

meter unit of measure in the metric system. A meter is about 39.37 inches.

millimeter unit of measure in the metric system. A millimeter is about 0.039 inches.

speedometer instrument that measures how fast a vehicle is moving

INDEX

calendar   12
compass   4, 5
direction   4
distance   14
length   7
measuring cup   10, 11
measuring tape   7
odometer   15
rain   11
rain gauge   11
ruler   6

speed   14
speedometer   15
time   12
weathervane   5
weight   8
yards   7